To Jo
With Love & Best Wishes
    from
    Alex, Grace,
        Bruce & Mhairi

Christmas 1988.

Cupar

in old picture postcards

by
Margaret W.W. Boyd

European Library - Zaltbommel/Netherlands MCMLXXXVII

GB   ISBN 90 288 3435 4 / CIP

© 1987 European Library - Zaltbommel/Netherlands

European Library in Zaltbommel/Netherlands publishes among other things the following series:

IN OLD PICTURE POSTCARDS *is a series of books which sets out to show what a particular place looked like and what life was like in Victorian and Edwardian times. A book about virtually every town in the United Kingdom is to be published in this series. By the end of this year about 300 different volumes will have appeared. 1,500 books have already been published devoted to the Netherlands with the title* **In oude ansichten.** *In Germany, Austria and Switzerland 650, 100 and 25 books have been published as* **In alten Ansichten;** *in France by the name* **En cartes postales anciennes** *and in Belgium as* **In oude prentkaarten** *and/or* **En cartes postales anciennes** *150 respectively 400 volumes have been published.*

For further particulars about published or forthcoming books, apply to your bookseller or direct to the publisher.

This edition has been printed and bound by Grafisch Bedrijf De Steigerpoort in Zaltbommel/Netherlands.

INTRODUCTION

For centuries past the importance of Cupar has been its geographical position. It is situated in the very middle of the backbone of the 'Kingdom of Fife' and is at the intersectional point of north, south, east and west. The land of Fife lay originally in the realm of Pictland, one of the two oldest of the four nations that emerged as northern Britain after the departure of the Romans in the fifh century. Obviously Cupar had its beginnings as a Pictish settlement in the early centuries A.D. Archaeological findings have proved that there were people living where Cupar is now in prehistoric times. There is no doubt that there must have been a fairly high eminence which made it ideal for a military station. The name 'Cupar' had a connection with this fact. The castle at Cupar developed from a Pictish fort which made it a vantage point in the defence of the inhabitants.

'Cupar' is a Celtic word. The derivation of its name has never been satisfactorily explained. One authority defines 'Cupar' the cup-like or hollow field, from 'cop' or 'cup' and 'ar' a field. Again it has been suggested that 'Cupar' is a composite name, consisting of two Gaelic words, 'cul' and 'bhar', 'cul' meaning the hinder back part and 'bhar' meaning an eminence. This eminence which is inferred in the name 'Cupar' is interesting geologically. It starts at the distance of nearly a quarter of a mile from the point where the Lady Burn meets the River Eden and it runs in a serpentine direction until it finishes on the Castle Hill or School Hill as it was once called. There is a point in the middle, higher than the rest which is called the Moot Hill where tradition says the Earls of Fife held their councils of war and dispensed justice. There is nothing artificial about the mound which is a natural deposit formed at some remote period and has been broken through by the action of the River Eden. On the north and south sides of the river, it has been reported, there was an immense bed of clay of very good quality which lent itself to the making of bricks and tiles. It was also suitable for the making of coarse earthenware.

Higher up behind this embankment lay the Wards, an extensive plain which was always under the plough. This plain was once the bottom of a large lake or basin which gradually emptied and became dried up by the wearing down of the embankment. The name 'Ferry' is still attached to some places on the sides of this plain. Up until the sixteenth century it was quite impassable. At the time of the Reformation when the army of the Lords of the Congregation faced the royal forces on the opposite side, this marsh was an insurmountable barrier between them.

Cupar ranks as one of the oldest royal burghs in Scotland. Its only existing charter dated 28th June 1382, was conferred by Robert II at Dunfermline. Cupar, however, was a royal burgh long before that date. Its first charter was probably conferred by David I, Malcolm IV or William the Lion.

Royal burghs were always near one of the king's castles. These castles were built at strategic points, commanding the main lines of communication which were the routes for peaceful merchants as well as for armed men.

The first castle at Cupar was probably erected in the eleventh century and was made of wood. It was not until the middle of the thirteenth century that wooden castles gave way to those of stone. The owner of the castle was a powerful ruler of a large area, responsible for helping the king in time of war. When he was away from home his wife looked after the stronghold for him. It has been recorded that the castle at Cupar was the scene of the death of Macduff's wife and children by order of Macbeth who ruled Scotland between 1040 and 1057. Macduff was the Thane of Fife who was absent from the castle in Cupar in support of Malcolm whose father Duncan had been murdered by Macbeth. Macduff eventually escaped to England and later helped Malcolm to return to Scotland to regain his crown. David de Wemyss is the first Sheriff of Fife to be recorded and his appointment is 1200. The importance of Cupar as a seat of justice is shown in records going back to 1239. The Justiciary of Fife held its courts on the Moat Hill (Mote Hill) which was called 'mons placite' or Statute Hill. The well-known saying 'Wha will to Cupar maun to Cupar' is of antique standing.

Royal burghs had specific rights of internal self-government for the purpose of internal or external trade. The old minutes of Cupar go back as far as 1549. An extract of one of these declares:

'The Burgh of Cupar has for magistrates, a Provost, three Bailies, a Dean of Guild and Treasurer. The Council consists of thirteen guild brethren and eight Deacons of Craft, one of whom must be Convener.' Cupar's burgesses had monopolistic rights over a large district of the county. They had overseas privileges as well. Trade with Flanders made Cupar more prosperous than some other royal burghs.

The burgh was an enclosed strong point. It was timbered and had a palisade. It had a fosse or earthen wall with 'ports' which were securely closed at night. The only means of entry was by one of these gates. There was a keeper at each one of these who always asked visitors what their business was. Unsatisfactory answers could take persons under suspicion to the magistrates who could order such people to be put in the town prison, a filthy cell under the level of the ground.

Building was mainly of wood and for poorer dwellings, of earth and turves. People were forbidden to carry lights from one house to another for fear of fire. The town in these far off days developed round the foot of the castle where the thane or sheriff lived. The town had probably one or two streets with wynds and closes on both sides of them. Shops were mainly booths which projected forward into the street. The town crier proclaimed the laws of the pasture lands or common. The town herd blew his horn every morning to let the animals know it was time to go to pasture and they knew the sound at once. Nearer the town were the town acres on which crops of oats, barley, peas and beans were grown.

The first parish church in Cupar was situated in the north of the town. It was dedicated to St. Mary and the saint's name accounts for 'Ladyburn', 'Ladywynd' and 'St. Mary's Road'. No trace of the church has been found. There are records of another church in the neighbourhood, that of St. Michael of Tarvit. This building was consecrated by Bishop de Bernham on 3rd April 1245. No trace of it remains now. It had an entirely separate existence until 1618 when it was united to the parish of Cupar.

Cupar at one time had a Dominican Monastery of Black Friars, situated at the foot of the castle. Amongst the lands held by the monks were four acres of arable land called St. Catherine's Haugh, the greater part of which later formed St. Catherine Street. It has been recorded that the monastery was used as a nursery for the royal children when the Stewart kings lived at Falkland Palace. In later times the monastery became the mansion of the Laird of Balgarvie. The building was finally removed when St. Catherine Street was opened up in the nineteenth century.

Cupar had two schools from an early period. One was a grammar school and the other a sang school. Sang schools were in existence primarily to teach music, and staff the church choirs. Generally, reading and writing were taught there as well and some sang schools taught Latin grammar. The sang school in Cupar in all probability was held in the Dominican Monastery by the monks. The location of the grammar school is unknown.

In 1415 Cupar was given a new church. The Church of St. Mary had fallen into a state of decay and a new place of worship was required. It was Bishop Wardlaw of St. Andrews who was responsible for the erection of a church on the site of the present Parish Church in the Kirkgate. It was built of polished freestone 133 feet long by 54 feet broad. At the western extremity of the church was a tower. In the tower was a heavy bell weighing 1 000 pounds which was called Michael. This church continued until 1785 when it was replaced by the building that exists today. The only parts of the fifteenth century building remaining are the tower and part of the session house. John Knox preached in the pre-Reformation building in 1560. One of the ministers of the Parish Church, Will Scott, a man of means and connected with the family of Balwearie, added a spire to the battlements of the church tower and paid for the building of it himself.

During the Protectorate Cromwell's troopers walked about the streets of Cupar and there may have been some marriages between them and local girls. It was during this time that Cupar was introduced to the doctrine of the Baptist Church. A Baptist preacher in Colonel Fairfax' regiment of foot, Mr. Browne, made a great impression on people in Cupar area. He was in the habit if re-baptizing several of the regiment in the River Eden 'neare to Erdries lodging, by dipping them in the water over head and eares, many of the inhabitants looking on'.

During the time of the Stewart kings Cupar was a corridor town between Falkland and St. Andrews. The townspeople were quite accustomed to see royal personnages and their retinues riding down the Bonnygate or Boudingait as it was then called on their way either to one place or another. Occasionally the royal parties broke their journeys at the Dominican Monastery for it was a two days' journey between Falkland and St. Andrews.

It was during the reign of James IV that trade was encouraged with Flanders. During his reign many Flemings came across to Scotland and settled in the country. They were the foreigners who taught trades and manufactures to the Scots. Cupar, as always, was an important trading town. In fact the Town Council was composed mainly of merchants whose power had increased during the century to the exclusion of the craftsmen. Many Flemish people had settled in and round about, to the royal burgh's advantage. The townspeople learned their crafts and made Cupar one of the principal weaving centres in northern Fife. On the farms round the town, fields of flax were grown which kept the spinners, weavers and waulkers busy. From cottages everywhere snatches of song could be heard as women chanted their rhythmic tunes to the sound of wheel and web.

The year 1490 saw the birth of David Lyndsay at one of his father's estates, the Mount, near Cupar. His family was descended from that of Lord Lindsay of the Byres in Haddingtonshire. He entered St. Andrews University in 1505 and left it in 1509. At the age of nineteen he entered the service of James IV and in 1512 became a page of honour to the young Prince James. He held this post until 1524 when he was dismissed with a pension by the four guardians of the young James who was now James V. Six years later he was appointed Lyon, King-at-Arms, and had a knighthood conferred on him. David Lyndsay was a man of many talents which were much appreciated by James V who sent him abroad on many missions. He was at the marriage of the King to Princess Madeleine, eldest daughter of Francis I,

King of France, which took place in Notre Dame in 1537. A year later, on 10th June, 1538, he awaited the arrival of James' second queen, Mary of Lorraine, beside his monarch, at Crail where she landed from France. He attended the royal couple in St. Andrews where they stayed for forty days 'with great merriness, sic as jousting on horses, and running at the lists, archery and hunting, and all other princely games. There-after the King and Queen went to Cupar in Fife and dined there and syne passed to Falkland.'

Sir David Lyndsay will always be remembered for his play 'The Three Estates'. It was first acted on 7th June, 1535, on the little hill in the centre of Cupar which until recently young boys and girls ascended and descended to and from the school there.

The town of Cupar in these far-off days was a busy one. Rich merchants, councillors, craftsmen and peasants mingled in the streets. A new street had been created in the burgh, that of the Kirkgait, the street in which the Parish Church was situated. Stone was some evidence in improvement in the town's buildings. Stone was beginning to replace wood in the building of houses. The houses of the merchant classes reflected the wealth and wide interests of their owners who had trading interests with the continent. Market stalls were still in evidence in the streets. The town's inhabitants were hard-working but they had their holy days or holidays on which they enjoyed all sorts of rustic frivolities. They were thrilled at the royal retinues that passed through the town, though, occasionally, they fled in terror to the safety of their homes when the sound of galloping horses proclaimed the approach of the wild Clephanes of Carslogie Castle and there they stayed until the horsemen had passed.

James V died in 1543, leaving as his heir a baby girl just a few days old. Scotland became thrown into a position only too familiar to the people. Who was to be regent? Two men wanted the position. One was the Earl of Arran and the other Cardinal Beaton. The former was the favourite. Arran was inclined to Protestantism and the other to Roman Catholicism. Arran favoured an alliance with England whereas Beaton favoured alliance with France. In no time the country was rent asunder by religious strife. Many Scots felt there was a need for reform within the Church. Then in 1554 the Queen Mother, Mary of Lorraine, became regent of Scotland and began to rule the country as if it were France. The young Queen Mary had been sent to France in 1548 and was betrothed to the Dauphin of that country. Between that date and the death of Mary of Lorraine in 1560 religious strife and intrigue ruled the land. On 13th June, 1559, Cupar Muir, situated quite close to Cupar, was the scene of a battle that never took place. The Lords of the Congregation who supported John Knox, that great champion of the Reformation in Scotland, had gathered a tremendous force occupying the sloping fields above the farm of Retreat and the present village of Cupar Muir. On the opposite side of the River Eden were the forces of the Queen Regent stretching as far as Tarvit Hill, along the bottom of Scotstarvit Hill and up by the Garlie Bank under the leadership of General D'Oisel. Surprised by the size of the Reformers' army, D'Oisel decided, after taking advice, to desist from engaging in battle and the army of the Congregation 're-turned to Couper, lauding and praising God for his mercie showed, and thairafter everie man to his dwelling place'.

Om 10th June, 1560, the Queen Regent died and a year later Queen Mary, no longer Queen of France on account of her husband's death, returned to Scotland. On 19th August, 1561, a ship brought her into the port of Leith. During her short reign she must have been a familiar figure to Cuparians for she loved to stay at Falkland Palace and often travelled between there and St. Andrews. She came specially to Cupar in 1562 and delighted the inhabitants with her beauty and charm as the townsfolk entertained her and showed, by the way they received her, their loyalty towards her. Six years later saw her defeat at the Battle of Langside and her flight into England. Scotland was again left in an unfortunate situation. Her son James had been proclaimed king but he was a mere infant.

Cupar as a corridor burgh between Falkland and St. Andrews must have seen many eminent men pass through its streets at this time and it could hardly help being affected by the rivalry of these great men for power during King James' minority. There were Archbishop Hamilton, the archbishop of St. Andrews whose palace was at Monimail not far to the west of Cupar, Sir James Melville, who was born at Halhill in 1535, situated not far from the royal burgh, William Kirkaldy of Grange, Scotland's best soldier, the Earl of Morton, a regent of great strength, and the 'Bonnie Earl o' Moray' who was so cruelly slain in 1592. When James VI escaped from Falkland Palace to his grand uncle, the Earl of March, awaiting him at St. Andrews, he must have ridden through Cupar, a young lad of sixteen years of age. In 1583 James held court at Cupar and this must have happened at what used to be known as Parliament Square, an old part of the town on the north side of the Kirkgait. Like his royal predecessors James often stayed at Falkland Palace before he left for England in 1603. He only once returned to the land of his birth after that date and that was in 1617.

Cupar did not change much between 1600 and 1700. The seventeenth century was a troublesome one. Religious strife and the rivalry of the nobility dominated the scene which made progress impossible. Charles I's attempts to introduce Episcopacy into Scotland produced the National Covenant of 1638 which was signed all over the country by those who were against Charles' religious changes for Scotland. His father James had had similar intentions which had brought as little unhappiness to Scotland and to the king himself. The minister of the Parish Church in Cupar at this time was Will Scott who played a prominent part in national ecclesiastical affairs. One of his great friends was Archbishop Spottiswoode of Dairsie who stayed in the castle there in his moments of leisure away from the worries of his office. It was Will Scott who added a spire to the battlements of the church tower in the Kirkgait. The great bell in the tower was also enlarged during his ministry. During his time as minister he lived at Belfield and went to church by an entrance from the south side through an elegant gate or door in the churchyard wall over which there was a fine arch. He is buried in the churchyard and his gravestone is still to be seen. It was also during his ministry in 1618 that the Church of St. Michael of Tarvit was united to the parish of Cupar and came under the care of the parish minister.

In 1627 Sir John Scott of Scotstarvit took up residence in Scotstarvit Tower. A Director of Chancery and a Lord of Session he was a man of great importance in Scotland. His name was well-known in literary circles in Europe, and his tower, a little to the south-west of Cupar, was familiar to continental students. To it came William Drummond of Hawthornden, Sir John's brother-in-law. Sir John is remembered as the first nobleman to project and finish the earliest topographical work on Scotland.

It is certain that when Charles I visited Scotland for his coronation in 1633 he also visited Falkland and St. Andrews. On one occasion he broke his journey at Cupar and 'dyned thair' and 'gat some dessert to his four houres in the Tolbooth'. It is also recorded that the local schoolmaster sang for his entertainment.

During the reign of Charles II the number of covenanters kept on increasing and in order to curb their activities and bring them to heel, punishment, meted out by the government, was severe indeed. David Haxton, an outstanding covenanter, had his home just a few miles out of Cupar. He was captured at Ayrsmoss in July 1680, taken to Edinburgh, tried and condemned to death. His execution was horrific. Parts of his body were sent all over Scotland. In the old churchyard behind the Parish Church in Cupar one of his hands is buried in the covenanters' grave there.

Two fires took place in Cupar during the 17th century, the first on 31 August 1616 and the second in April 1669. The years between 1651 and 1690 were plague years in Scotland and the 1680's produced severe famines. Fife, however, produced the two best doctors in the land, Archibald Pitcairne and Sir Robert Sibbald. The former was a descendant of the ancient family of Pitcairne in Fife and the latter was born at Over Rankeilour in 1641, a descendant of the Sibbalds of Balgonie. It is recorded that it was due to his perseverance that the Royal College of Physicians of Edinburgh obtained its charter of incorporation. Knighted by James, Duke of York, in 1682 he became the first Professor of Medicine at Edinburgh University in 1685. In 1710 his 'History of Fife' was published, a later edition being published in Cupar in 1803 by Robert Tullis.

There is evidence that, in the 17th century in Cupar, horse races were run every year in the month of April. These races took place somewhere in the Tarvit area and lasted over a period of two days.

It was at the end of the seventeenth century that the Scottish Episcopalians in Cupar left the Parish Church and met as a body in a meeting place in the Bonnygate, the site of which later became the first post office. The Scottish Episcopalians were strong Jacobites and when James VII fled to France they continued to pray for the King 'o'er the Water'. A Convention of Estates, to counter this, proclaimed that all ministers of the gospel had to pray for King William and Queen Mary. The Reverend Alexander Lundie of the Parish Church was one of four hundred ministers who refused to do so. He was ejected from the Church for his sins but there can be no doubt, however, that he had a certain care over this group which left the Parish Church with him.

The eighteenth century is an important one for Scotland. It is a period full of activity which witnessed many changes. Like towns all over Scotland and England, Cuparians heard four royal proclamations of succession at the Mercat Cross. When Queen Anne died in 1702 a new royal house came into being, that of Hanover. Her successor was George I who was not welcomed by the Jacobites in Scotland. The rising of 1715 in support of James VII's heir, the 'Pretender' was a failure. Another attempt to restore the Stewarts to the throne was made in 1745 but it, too, was unsuccessful. On his return to London from the disastrous field of Culloden, the Duke of Cumberland, in charge of the royal army, committed terrible destruction in the Episcopalian chapel in the Bonnygate at Cupar. The altar, pulpit, seats and service books were taken into the street and burned, the English soldiers shouting, joking and kicking the objects into the flames while the frightened citizens were helpless to do anything about it.

Fife had many loyal Jacobites. One of these was Arthur, Baron Balmerino. It is recorded that in 1745 he declared James VIII as king with great solemnity at the Mercat Cross in Cupar. Like many of the nobility of the time he had a town house in Cupar the site of which is still preserved by the name of Balmerino Place. The Earl of Crawford had his town house where St. John's Church stands and the Earl of Rothes had his in the Millgate. Winthank House in the Kirk Wynd was the town residence of the family of Wemyss of Unthank.

Cupar was one of five flourishing towns in Fife in the sixteenth century that had a grammar school which had quite a reputation. It also had a 'Sang Schule'. These schools were maintained by Cupar Town Council. It is not known where these first schools were but in 1727 Cupar got a new school. It was built on the Castlehill and stands there to this day. The building was divided into two compartments which had separate entries, one to the front of the building and one at the back. The two compartments had no communication with each other. In the one was taught French, Latin, geography etc. and in the other, English, writing, arithmetic, book-keeping, meusuration etc. The 1727 school produced four scholars who brought honour to their teachers and to the town. They were, in order of age, John Campbell, who became Lord Chief Justice of England, the younger son of Dr. Campbell, minister of the Parish Church, whose memory is still preserved by the name of the house in the Crossgate where he was born which is always referred to as the Chancellor's House; Alexander Berry, born at Hilltarvit Farm, a man of many talents, settler, farmer, merchant, politician, philanthropist and reformer whose name lives on in New South Wales; George Walker, born at Hilton of Pitblado who became a church minister and although he spent the fifty-five years of his ministry in the church of Kinnell in Angus he will always be remembered for his pastorship, his scholarship, his authorship and his services to the Church in general; David Wilkie, third son of the Reverend David Wilkie, minister of Cults, who became an artist of international fame.

The eighteenth century saw a break-away from the Established Church. The forming of another presbytery brought about the first Secession. In Cupar a group of Seceders acquired a piece of land in the town on which was built their church, the Boston Church, after Thomas Boston, one of the principal ministers connected with the movement. Sometimes it was referred to as the West Church. Although it is no longer a church, the building exists today and is used as a bingo hall. In 1752 there was a further rupture within the Scottish Church. The second Secession was known as the Relief (Relief from the burden of Patronage). A group was formed in Cupar and eventually in 1796 the Burnside Church was ready to hold the congregation. In 1799 a small session house was added. Later the session house was taken down and replaced by a comfortable little hall which later became a coach house in connection with the Burnside Hotel.

In 1785, 370 years after the building of the 1415 church in the Kirkgate, it was decided to pull down the fabric of the building and erect a new church in its place. The new church which exists today is a plain building, lacking any of the elegance of the previous one, the old church of St. Christopher. The tower and spire belonging to the 1415 building have been preserved and are a great ornament to the town. The present Session house is still part of the original building and portions of the arches of the 1415 erection can still be traced.

The Episcopalian chapel has already been mentioned. It was situated in the Bonnygate on the site of the first post office in Cupar. Reverend Alexander Lundie was the first minister and there is no record of any other until 1743. Sometime during the eighteenth century the congregation left the Bonnygate chapel which was ransacked by the Duke of Cumberland during the Jacobite rebellion of 1745. A hall was acquired in the Crossgate, the premises of which were called the 'Temple Buildings'.

In the autumn of the same year that Cupar built its second Parish Church, 1785, it had a strange accidental visitor in the person of Vincenzo Lunardi, an Italian aeronaut. As he crossed the Firth of Forth in his balloon it got out of control and came down in a field near Coaltown of Callange. His landing caused quite a stir in the neighbourhood and he found himself welcomed and acclaimed by everyone. Cupar entertained him, the Provost and Magistrates inviting him to dine and presenting him with the freedom of the Burgh. The ladies of the town repaired his balloon and in recompense for their labours he gave each of them a piece of the balloon as a memento. He was also honoured by a visit of Lord Balgonie, the heir of the sixth Earl of Leven and fifth Earl of Melville whose home was at Melville House. The name of Lunardi has been preserved for posterity in the name given to one of the new housing sites in the town.

Between 1750 and 1800 a new prosperity and activity had shown itself in Scotland due to the fact that the country in general had begun to find peace and security after the long period of internal strife and struggle. There was not a little invention especially in agricultural implements and there were the chemical experiments of Joseph Black and his followers in the province of bleaching. This research was going to have a great effect on the paper trade. By the end of the eighteenth century there were several paper mills situated round the administrative centres of the country. In Fife there was only one paper mill when Robert Tullis took possession of the property in 1809. Robert came to Cupar in 1800 and stayed for the rest of his life. In 1801 he bought property in the Bonnygate which he enlarged and altered. His shop was in the front and the printing press behind. He himself lived in the flat above. Later these premises became the business quarters of Messrs. J. & G. Innes which changed hands in the middle of the present century. Between 1803 and 1808 some very famous classics were printed by Tullis. Robert was interested in other affairs outside his business. A member of the Magistracy of Cupar Town Council he was made a Freeman of the Burgh in 1817. He was also a Captain in the Fife Militia. In the year 1822 Robert founded the first Fife County Newspaper, the 'Cupar Herald' of 'Fife, Kinross, Strathearn and Clackmannan Advertiser'. A year later it was renamed the 'Fife Herald'. The first number of the 'Cupar Herald' was published on 14th March 1822, printed on hand-made paper from Auchmuty. It was circulated free of charge and did not have the 4d tax stamp which succeeding numbers carried on the front page. The selling price of the paper which consisted of two folded sheets was 7d a copy. Two persons were involved in the printing of it which was done on an old wooden press at the rate of fifty copies per hour.

The opening of the nineteenth century saw the beginning of the Napoleonic Wars. Britain was busily preparing for a French invasion and all over the country there were signs of the erection of adequate defences against such a happening. In Cupar Volunteers drilled on the Big Common and in 1803 it had its Militia. During the time of the Peninsular War a hero emerged in the person of John, fourth Earl of Hopetoun, whose residence was at Over Rankeilour, a well-known mansion, a few miles to the west of Cupar. For his ability at the Battle of Corunna he was invested with the Order of the Bath. It is interesting to note that after the Battle of Waterloo, Napoleon's plans to escape by sea were hindered by a distinguished naval officer Sir Frederick Lewis Maitland, Captain of the warship Bellerophon to whom Napoleon surrendered himself. Sir Frederick was born at Nether Rankeilour, an estate not far from the royal burgh of Cupar.

In 1820 George III died and the royal proclamation of succession by the Sheriff-Substitute was read at three different places at Cupar. There was a special processional order which had to be adhered to, which started at the Tontine Hotel in St. Catherine Street. The three places were the Mercat Cross, opposite the Post Office and opposite the New Bridge. The Post Office was in the Bonnygate and the New Bridge was in what is now Station Road. At each of these places a circle was formed by each of the different trades within which the Sheriff-Substitute stood. He was given a response by the people assembled with three times three cheers, the band playing 'God Save the King'. The ceremony ended with the staff of the County Militia firing a feu-de-joie while the band played the anthem.

A few changes took place in the town within the first twenty-five years of the nineteenth century. In 1812 the Mercat Cross was removed from its position in the centre of the town and taken to Wemysshall Hill. A year later the Tolbooth or prison which stretched far across towards the foot of the Castlehill was cleverly demolished by Provost Ferguson in face of great opposition. The building was burned to the ground in an all-night operation and after its removal a lovely new street was planned, and named St. Catherine Street, in remembrance of the monastery which had stood on that site in centuries long past. One of the new buildings in the street was an Episcopal chapel erected in 1823. Up to that time the Episcopalian congregation had worshipped in a hall in the Crossgate. In addition to the chapel there were the new County Buildings. In the County Hall were some fine portraits. One of these was of Thomas Erskine, ninth Earl of Kellie, Lord Lieutenant of the County of Fife, the work of David Wilkie, done in 1828. At the corner of St. Catherine Street and Crossgate was the Town-House. Both the County Buildings and Town-House were begun in 1817. A new gaol was found on the north bank of the Eden opposite the foot of St. Catherine Street which the building was to enhance. It was from this prison, on 30th September 1830, that John Henderson was hanged for his murder of a weaver, Millie by name, who resided at Whinny Park, a small feu on the estate of the Earl of Leven, on the road between Monimail and Collessie.

In September 1826 a tower was completed on the Mount Hill in remembrance of the Earl of Hopetoun for the distinguished service he had given his country. The monument is a definite landmark in the area, a constant reminder of one of Britain's most famous soldiers and great men.

In 1830 George IV died and was succeeded by William IV. For the second time in ten years a new monarch was proclaimed in Cupar. In less than seven years there was a third proclamation, that of Queen Victoria which took place in Cupar on Saturday 24th June 1837.

At the beginning of the nineteenth century there were five places of worship in Cupar, the Parish Church in the Kirkgate, the First Relief Church at the Westport, the Burnside Church, the Relief Church in the Provost Wynd and the Episcopalian Chapel in the Bonnygate. The latter place of worship was removed first to the Crossgate and then to St. Cathearine Street. Now as the century proceeded, a few changes for places of worship took place. On Christmas Eve 1837 an additional new church building to house the overflow from the Parish Church was opened at the Bonnygate end of North Union Street. It was called St. Michael's Church. In 1821 the Baptists began to worship in the Kirkgate Chapel. The Baptist preacher, Mr. Watson, had found the money for such a place by going on a preaching tour. This chapel served the Baptists until 1848 when they moved into a building in the Provost Wynd which had been used since 1830 by a dissenting body from the Boston Church which had decided to cease functioning. On 16th December 1866, a new church was opened in the Bonnygate for the congregation which had worshipped in the Burnside.

In the same year a new Episcopalian Chapel was built for the growing Episcopalian congregation in Cupar. It only increased the sittings by sixty or seventy and the unfortunate thing about the new church was that there was no room for extension.

The Disruption of 1843 brought about a division in the Established Church throughout Scotland. In Cupar the seceders acquired a place of worship in South Union Street and later in 1878 a fine building was erected in the Bonnygate called St. John's.

It was not until 1864 that a small chapel was erected in the Millgate for the small group of Catholics in Cupar Parish which numbered between 150 and 200. Its erection was due to Mr. William Douglas-Dick of Montrave who bought the site for the chapel and between 1864 and 1870 maintained a resident priest.

In 1843 Cupar acquired a new jail. Its site was in the north-east of the Braehead district. It took the place of the jail which had been erected on the north bank of the Eden opposite the foot of St. Catherine Street. This building which today belongs to the firm of William Watt, seedsman, had never been satisfactory. This new 1843 jail acted in that capacity until 1888. It was from this building that two brothers, Michael and Peter Scanlan, were taken to the Fluthers to be hanged for murder, on 5th July, 1852. It was the last public hanging to take place in Cupar. After 1888 the Braehead building became a military barracks. During the Second World War it was used as a prison again by the Polish Forces stationed in Cupar area. The walls are very strong and it is their structural strength that has made demolition impossible and so the building has survived.

The first attempt at constructing a railway in Fife was made in 1841. In 1847 a line from Burntisland to Cupar was completed and in 1848 a line from Cupar to Tayport was opened. Later the Tay and Forth bridges greatly improved the quickness and comfort of main line travel and made Dundee and Edinburgh attractive centres for shopping and education. It was due to Mr. Maitland Makgill Crichton of Nether Rankeilour who achieved the railway bridge for Cupar instead of a level crossing. His statue can be seen near the top of the railway bridge.

The nineteenth century made great advances in education and during it there were many opportunities for learning in the town. It has already been recorded that Cupar had a burgh school of some importance in the fourteenth century. This school lasted into the eighteenth century when in 1727 a new school was erected by the Town Council. The building stands there today. In 1823 it became known as Madras Academy. During the nineteenth century extensions and improvements were made. An old building which stood in the middle of the front playground was removed and the children who were educated there were transferred to the Kirkgate School or Kirkgate Madras as it was called in the 1860's. Later in 1881 an extension was built on to Kirkgate Madras.

Besides the Academy there were other schools or independent establishments. One of these was run by the Misses Adamson who owned a mantua and millinery establishment. They taught dressmaking and millinery to girls of a certain class who had attended the Burgh School for a few years. From the Misses Adamson's establishment these girls proceeded to another school run by the Misses McPherson who taught refinement of manners, deportment and fine needlework. They also made a specialty of French pronunciation.

Henrietta Keddie of literary fame and her sister Margaret ran a private school for girls at Westfield House for twenty years. When they gave up the school in 1869 a girls' school was opened a year later almost opposite Westfield House. The school was built by money gifted by Lady Baxter of Kilmaron Castle, the wife of Sir David Baxter, Bart. of Kilmaron and Balgarvie.

Yet another girls' school, Bonvil School, must be mentioned. It was situated on the north side of Carslogie Road. The headmistress, Miss Hogben, and her staff aimed at equipping their young ladies with an education expected of girls from high class homes. This school was a boarding establishment.

In addition to the above there were other independent or 'adventure' schools in the burgh which gave satisfactory instruction to their young pupils. It was obvious that the folk in the royal burgh attached much importance to education.

The nineteenth century was a flourishing period for Cupar. There were eight incorporated trades in the town, weavers, hammermen, bakers, fleshers, tailors, shoemakers, wrights, masons and waulkers. There were a few charitable societies, all beneficent bodies. There were four masonic lodges, and there was in addition the Lomond grand encampment of Knights Templars No. 30.

Cupar's first bank was opened in 1787, a branch of the Bank of Scotland. In 1792 a branch of the British Linen Bank was established in the town. In 1802 a group of gentlemen initiated the Cupar Bank and in 1803 another group started the Fife Bank. In 1812 the Commercial Bank of Scotland was established but by 1840 the only two banking establishments in Cupar were the branches of the British Linen Company and the Commercial Bank. A Savings Bank had been established in the 1830's but it had not been successful.

The principal manufactures in Cupar were those of linen weaving and spinning of yarn. There were three mills for the spinning of yarn, a flax mill, another mill where yarn was spun and thread twisted. There were two plash mills. Other industries in the town were concerned with the milling of corn, flour and barley. There was a snuff mill in the Lebanon. Cupar had two tanworks and glue was manufactured in the town. There were three breweries. A Brick and Tile Work operated at Cupar Muir. There was a rope-work in the Crossgate. Six quarries existed in Cupar Parish, four of which were of excellent sandstone.

Cupar was a leading and important market town in the

nineteenth century. Market day in Cupar used to be Thursday until it was changed to Tuesday in 1850. In 1880 premises were acquired near the railway station which became the site of the present auction market. These were acquired by Messrs. Speedie Bros. in 1888 which firm still owns them.

A pipe-clay factory was started in Cupar in the 1870's, a small family affair of which there were many in the town. In 1862 it is recorded that there were forty-six grocers' shops in Cupar, two carriage works, several joiners' shops, three tinsmiths, a cooperage and an aerated water factory. There were twelve smithies in the parish and a foundry. Gaslight was first supplied in Cupar in 1830.

During the nineteenth century some new housing was erected, mainly in the east of the burgh. A group of houses in the South Road, the Knox Cottages, was built. Three new buildings came into being, the Corn Exchange in 1861, the Duncan Institute 1870 and the Sunday School Hall in the Kirk Wynd which was made possible by Mr. John Pitcairn of Pitcullo during the ministry of the Reverend Dr. James Cochrane.

For a town of its size Cupar had an amazing social life during the century. There were many societies. It had a lending library. When the Guild Hall was completed in 1845 it offered accommodation for various purposes including that of a theatre on certain occasions. Sport was not forgotten either. In 1856 there was a golf course at Tailabout. Tarvit Pond accommodated curlers and the Carthaugh was flooded for the first time for skating in 1852. Cupar Cricket Club which was founded in the early years of the century acquired its own site in Bonvil Park in 1884. There were two bowling greens, one in the station area, and the other in the Kirkgate, before the time of the Duncan Institute. The River Eden attracted many fine anglers. Trout was moderately plentiful and larger catches were quite possible.

The century had its bad patches which were reflected in the life of the burgh. There were times when Cupar was visited by typhus in 1838 and 1847, by cholera in 1832 and 1854 and by smallpox in 1862. The century began with war which did not finish until 1815. Half-way through, in 1854, the Crimean War began and before the century's close there was the Boer War which continued into the twentieth century. The start of the century saw the death of Queen Victoria on 22nd January 1901. She had reigned for sixty-four years. Just a few years before, the country had commemorated her Diamond Jubilee. Cupar's Provost McQueen, his magistrates and councillors, with the backing of the townspeople, had celebrated the occasion by bringing back the old Mercat Cross of the royal burgh from Wemysshall Hill to the site on which it stands today after an absence of eighty years.

The announcement of Edward VII's accession was a little different from that on previous occasions. The new position of the Mercat Cross made it a natural platform for such scenes of historic pageantry and the wide expanse in front a natural auditorium. Provost Watson stood beside Sheriff Armour in his splendid robes, wearing the fine gold chain of his office which had been worn for the first time at Queen Victoria's Golden Jubilee in 1887 by Provost James Hain. Every link of the chain bears the names and dates of Cupar's provosts and the beautiful medallion has the town's old coat-of-arms engraved on it.

Edward's coronation should have taken place on 26th June 1902, for which date all preparations had been made. The King's sudden illness which necessitated an operation postponed the ceremony until the month of August. Hostilities in South Africa had been concluded in May 1902 with the signing of the Treaty of Pretoria just a few weeks before the King's Coronation.

In 1904 the Adamson Cottage Hospital was opened. Two other items of interest for Cuparians took place that year. Thomas Barclay, the eldest son of Dr. George Barclay, barrister and laird of Bonvil (Bonvil House is now known as Rathcluan), who had received his early education at Madras Academy, was given a knighthood on the King's birthday and later he obtained an officership of the Legion of Honour. Another Cuparian, Henrietta Keddie, daughter of Philip Keddie, a lawyer in Cupar, was given a royal literary pension. Her nom-de-plume was Sarah Tytler. A prolific writer she is known best for her look 'Three Generations' which was published in 1911.

1905 was the year of an election in East Fife. The Unionist candidate was Captain John Gilmour of Woodburne, Ceres. Although he put up a good fight he lost to his opponent who was none other than Mr. Asquith. 1909 saw the installation of a Master of the Provincial Grand Lodge of Fife and Kinross, Mr. Henry Hilton Brown, in the County Hall, Cupar and the presentation of colours to the Fife and Forfar Yeomanry. This latter event was a unique occasion in the town. The presentation of the Guidon to the Regiment was performed by the Lord Lieutenant of the County, the Earl of Elgin and Kincardine. 1910 saw the death of King Edward and the succession of his son George V. His coronation took place in 1911.

In 1910 Cupar Town Council was made a gift of Bonvil House and Bonvil Park which had been the property of Mr. George Barclay, L.L.D. who had died. The house and lands were bought by Mr. John C. Duffus, son of Mr. James Duffus, Westport House, who presented them to the Council on condition that the Park was called Duffus Park. In the same year Captain John Gilmour of Woodburne, Ceres, was returned M.P. for East Renfrewshire.

1911 saw the Cupar Branch of the Scottish Wholesale Society move into new quarters at 99 Bonnygate, and a new First Magistrate of the town in the person of Provost Stark, one of Cupar's finest leaders. During the first year of his office the Royal Highland Show took place in the County Town. It was held on 9th, 10th, 11th and 12th July and its site was the estate of Kinloss owned by Mrs. M.H. Addison-Scott.

Two other interesting events took place in 1912. On 20th September Sir James Low of Kilmaron Castle marked the coming-of-age of his son and heir, James Morrison Low, by a memorable fête at the castle and on 24th October a son and heir was born to Captain John Gilmour, M.P. younger, of Montrave.

On 2nd June 1914, Dr. John Alexander Robertson, dentist, died. He had reached the age of 89 and had practised in Fife for fifty years. Dr. Robertson had studied dentistry both in London and America and it was while he was there that he saw how teeth could be extracted by the use of nitrous-oxide gas. When he re-

turned to Scotland just before the outbreak of the American Civil War, he with Mr. Campbell of Dundee, the father of Dr. Graham Campbell of Cupar Amateur Opera fame, was the first to introduce anaesthetics in the extraction of teeth in this part of the country. Profiting by American experience, Dr. Robertson had brought with him forceps designed for every human tooth. With these advantages he built up a practice which took him all over East Fife.

1914, a fateful year, saw Britain declare war on Germany. The date was 4th August. For the next four years the war continued. Cupar, as everywhere else, was engaged during that period raising funds for the war effort. 1916, a critical year, was an anxious one for Britain. Special church services were held everywhere. There was a weather incident in Cupar that year which had never been witnessed before. In July there was an unprecedented rainfall which caused extensive flooding. The Burnside in Cupar became a loch and a boat carried people from one side to another. School children living in the Newtown and in the north of Cupar had to cross by boat to the foot of the Ladywynd to get to school which was not at Castlehill for during wartime the school had been taken over by troops, and classes were held in St. John's Church.

With the entrance of America into the war the Germans made a violent effort to win a victory in the west before the arrival of the Americans. A massed offensive against the British began. Bit by bit the Allies kept piercing the German line. By 8th August 1918, Germany was faced with surrender. On 11th November Germany was granted an armistice and the war was over. The adjustment to peace had to take time. In Cupar as indeed all over the country there were troops everywhere. It took time to empty halls. Returning warriors arrived back slowly but their welcome was one of joy and extreme gladness. There was just sheer thankfulness to be at peace again after the long dark years of struggle.

On 10th May 1919, Field Marshall Sir Douglas Haig was made a freeman of the burgh and three years later, on 29th April 1922, he returned to Cupar to unveil the War Memorial. In 1923

Queen Mary visited Cupar and laid a wreath on the Memorial. The following year a marble slab was unveiled there to commemorate her visit. Provost R.O. Pagan had succeeded Provost Stark in 1922 and during his occupation of the civic chair fifty Weir Steel houses were erected in Cupar and a further Housing (Brick) Scheme was built at Westport. Provost Pagan saw the transfer of Bell Baxter school to Fife Education Authority. It was at the beginning of the Provostship of Mr. H.J. Smith in 1926 that Cupar's Beet Factory was opened.

On 6th November 1924 Sir John Gilmour of Montrave was appointed first Secretary of State for Scotland and two years later the status of Scottish Secretary was raised to that of Secretary of State for Scotland, entitling the holder to a seat in the Cabinet. Sir John was sworn in by H.M. King George V on 26th July 1926. Later, on 29th September, he played himself in as Captain of the Royal and Ancient Golf Club, St. Andrews and on 30th October he was elected Lord Rector of the University of Edinburgh.

1926 was the year of the General Strike. The spirit of the Nation and solidarity of the people shone brightly through the depression and there was a rally by the people to the message of the broadcast of the Prime Minister, Mr. Baldwin, whose wise counsel to the country was to 'keep steady'.

Up to 1914 Cupar had not altered much from what it had been a century before. No new industries had been introduced but many old industries had disappeared. Buildings belonging to the latter, were in a state of disrepair and dereliction. Many families lived in closes in the town in poor conditions. As has already been stated, some attempt after the war had been made to improve housing conditions. In 1926 a bandstand was erected in the Hood Park, made possible by a bequest from Miss Anne Black of Castlebank. In 1925 the Tontine Hotel was demolished to make room for the extension of the County Buildings. The opening of the Beet Factory took place on 8th November 1926. The ceremony was performed by Lady Gilmour, second wife of Sir John Gilmour, Secretary of State for Scotland.

Another newcomer to Cupar was the trans-Atlantic wireless station which was established at Kemback in 1927 and five years later was transferred to Cairngreen. In 1929 a new reservoir was built at Garliebank which had a capacity of 200,000 gallons, enough to provide a circulair water supply. On 24th August 1925 the machinery at the old Lucklawhill Quarry, near Balmullo, was put in motion and on 28th September 1929 the new Lime Works at Cults were opened by Lady Cochrane. On 19th June 1930 a centenary luncheon of Cupar Gas Company Ltd. was held in the Royal Hotel. At Riggs Place a laundry owned by Mr. W.D. Brownlee became a valuable addition to the industrial life of Cupar. The very latest machinery had been installed and motor vans collected goods from all over East Fife.

There were few cars in the twenties. Transport was mainly by horse. Sheep and cattle were brought into the town by stockmen. Farm servants moved house either at the May or November terms. Opportunities for them to change their employers were possible at feeing markets held at certain times of the year.

By 1930 Cupar had re-organised itself and was back to normal. It had to a certain extent sloughed off the inhibiting effects of the war years. Its recreational activities were surprising. It had much to offer in the way of sport. It had one of the finest public parks in the country with an outstanding Cricket Club, grass tennis courts and four new hard courts situated in the space formerly occupied at Bonvillette by the Football Club which were opened by Mr. J.C. Duffus on 6th June 1925. In 1925 Mr. Duffus bought an adjacent park and donated it to provide football facilities. In 1927 his services to his native town were recognised when he was made a freeman of the royal burgh. His signature followed that of Earl Haig of Bemersyde. In 1927 Mr. Duffus' sister, Miss Euphemia Duffus, further enhanced the public park by the erection of a lodge, the residence of the park ranger.

It was in the twenties, however, that Cupar found a new entertainment. Two cinemas came into existence. Union Street Hall which was first a church and then a meeting place became the 'Musketeers' Theatre'. The second cinema was called 'La Scala'. It had originally been the Boston Church which was discontinued for religious worship after the First World War. Both cinemas presented silent films until the advent of the 'Talkies'. 1932 saw a new extension erected at Bell Baxter School to house Advanced Division, pupils who up until that year had taken the course at Castlehill. The old buildings were entirely remodelled and new rooms added. Part of the additions housed an agricultural section. The school was opened by the Earl of Elgin on 30th June 1932. Kirkgate School which had catered for infant children for many decades now became a domestic science department for Bell Baxter and the infant children were transferred to Castlehill which now became a purely primary school. The development of wireless opened up a whole new field of happiness. Radio and broadcast wireless brought music and entertainment into the home. On Christmas Day 1934 King George V sent a message to his people from his microphone at Buckingham Palace which was heard in all parts of the Empire. In 1935 King George and Queen Mary celebrated their Silver Jubilee and Cupar like the rest of the country rejoiced with them. 1936 had scarcely begun when King George died at Sandringham on 20th January at the age of seventy. At the Mercat Cross in Cupar Provost Russell proclaimed the accession of the new monarch and before the year was out he had to read the Proclamation of another sovereign, that of King George VI. Provost Russell was the only civic head to have read the Proclamations of two monarchs in the same year. The coronation of George VI took place on 12th May 1937. Cupar, like every town and village in the country, rose to the occasion. The new reign was to begin with a period of uncertainty and anxiety. Adolf Hitler's moves since his coming to power in Germany in the early thirties began to fill Europe with fear of war. Britain became alerted. The Navy was mobilised. Gas masks were issued and trenches were being dug against aerial attack. In 1938 it seemed that war might be avoided. When Hitler attacked Poland in August 1939 Great Britain was forced to declare war on Germany as did France, for both countries had promised to support Poland. Suddenly the ordinary life of the country seemed to cease, disrupted by war conditions. Young men were called up. Young women were also volunteering for service. Recreational life became geared to fund-raising for Red Cross and comforts for the troops. A.R.P. posts had to be constantly manned. Home Guard duties had to be maintained. Homes were being shared by children evacuated from the cities. Schools had to accommodate evacuated children and their teachers which meant part-time teaching. At night all homes had to have windows blacked out and street wardens were perpetually on guard, in the space of months the life of the country had undergone a sensational change.

For the next five years Britain endured a period of time fraught with anxiety. The first years of the war were, indeed, fearful for the Allies. The German Army seemed to have every advantage on its side. Then a great victory of the Eighth Army in Egypt and Libya revived hopes among the Allies. The sound of church bells pealed out from churches in Britain on 18th November 1943, in honour of the event. On that morning, the cheering sound of the bells of the Parish Church and St. John's Church in Cupar again summoned people to worship after having been silent for two years. It was at the beginning of the War that Cupar once again saw foreign troops in her midst. This time the soldiers were from Poland. During their stay in Cupar many friendships were made and towards the end of 1942 a Scottish Polish Society was started in the town. It was after five years and 246 days of the most bitter struggle in history that the Second World War was terminated. The 8th May 1945, was Victory Day in Europe. All over the country decorated buildings and marvellous displays of colour were everywhere. Churches held special thanksgiving services. There were two days of public holidays. Offices and schools were closed. Everywhere there were signs of thankfulness and gratitude that hostilities were at an end and normal life could begin once more. During that period of war many well-known men and women in Cupar had died, who had served their town well. Now many young men and women were returning to their home town to continue where they had left off. After a period of adjustment normality took over again. At the East Fife Election in July 1945, Mr. J. Henderson Stewart was re-elected.

In November of the same year Treasurer R.G. Brown accepted the provostship of Cupar in succession to Provost Faichney.

In October 1946 two new restaurants were established in the basement of the County Buildings. The new premises occupy that part formerly used by A.R.P. during wartime. One of these can cater for eighty persons and the other is a fitting place for very special visitors to the County Council on official business. The old names 'Tontine' and 'Tolbooth' have been retained for these fine additions to the County Offices. Another restaurant was opened in Cupar in April 1946, the New Oak Room in Elder's Café in St. Catherine Street. In May 1947 Cupar's new Bowling Club at Duffus Park was opened by Mrs. M.M. Gold, the donor of this fine addition to an already well-equipped park. In November 1947, the wedding took place of Princess Elizabeth and Lieutenant Philip Mountbatten, Duke of Edinburgh. In Cupar the County Buildings, Town Hall and several other properties' staffs were given the opportunity of hearing the wedding broadcast. Schools were on holiday and flags were flying in various places in the town. In June 1948 King George VI, Queen Elizabeth and Princess Margaret paid a visit to Cupar. The county town rose to the royal occasion and made the visit a memorable one for the town's records.

In October 1948 the Flax Factory at Uthrogle which had operated during the war years, was taken over by Messrs. A & R Scott Ltd., West Mills, Colinton, Midlothian, makers of the well-known Porage Oats. The site of the factory at Uthrogle had served some years before as the venue for Fife Foxhounds' point-to-point races and the judges' box was still visible until quite recent times.

Since 1950 great changes have taken place in Cupar. The Bonnygate, Crossgate and Kirkgate, the three original streets of the burgh, to all appearances remain the same but beyond these the whole character of the old town has changed.

In 1953 Cupar gained a new provost in succession to Provost Brown. Provost Andrew Mitchell Scott was to keep the provostship for over twenty years and during his administration the town's appearance altered considerably. This change was most noticeable in the new housing areas that have sprung up in all directions from the centre of the town. Tarvit House was demolished early in the second half of the century and an extensive housing site in the area almost resembled a new town on the southern side of the railway station. Sandylands Road site between the Golf Course and the foot of the Garliebank was also extensive. Towards the west of the town new houses appeared at Ferryfield. In the north of the town appeared Kinloss Crescent, Kinloss Park, Kilmaron Drive and Crescent and recently a large independent housing scheme has been erected on the north side of the Eden to the left of the St. Andrews Road. Another site is in preparation to the right of the road. Housing schemes, both independent and council controlled, have appeared over the last twenty or thirty years and the project is never ending. Cupar's central position makes it an excellent centre for business people wishing to live away from their places of business. The town also is well-placed for travelling to the cities, the seaside and the Highlands.

The town itself has much to offer its residents. There is a good variety of shops and several supermarkets. There are many societies suiting the tastes of most people and the Duncan Institute offers an excellent library service. Sports facilities are excellent. Bowling, tennis, cricket and putting can be had in the Duffus Park and football and rugby are played on the park's extension. Elmwood College, the fine further education centre at the western limit of the town provides access to the swimming pool and saunas that were opened just a year or two ago. There is an excellent sports centre in the East Road, fishing in the Eden and a golf course in the south-east of the town.

Educational facilities for a town of Cupar's size are outstanding. In 1975 a new primary school was opened in Ceres Road, to take the place of the Castlehill building which now operates as a community centre. A fine Infant School was opened in 1951 in Westfield Road to house the town's five-to-seven year olds. Just recently a nursery school was erected on its site to take care of pre-school children. Several playgroups also cater for the three-to-five year olds. Bell Baxter School takes care of secondary children. The old building with the 1932 extension and the new building to the west of the town comprise the whole secondary unit. In addition the Catholic children have their own building in the Millgate and there are two special schools, one in the Perth Road and the other at Dalgairn.

There are many small businesses in Cupar. Law firms, building societies and insurance offices abound. The closing of the Beet Factory in the seventies was a death blow to the town which has not been remedied so far although the site houses many various firms which have taken up space there over the recent years. Agriculture is still a very important industry in Cupar District. The Corn Exchange which was renovated and made into two fine halls is still the meeting place for farmers on market days and the auction mart off Station Road does not lack business on weekly market occasions.

The County Buildings in St. Catherine Street until 1975 were the hub of Fife County but since the arrival of regionalisation, they have become the headquarters of North East Fife District Council.

Over the past thirty years there have been changes in the churches. The first change came just after the middle of the century when St. Michael's Church was taken over by the Education Authority, becoming an assembly hall and gymnasium for Bell Baxter School. In 1965 a new Catholic Church was opened in the Kirkgate. The Baptist Church has disappeared in the Provost Wynd and its members now worship in what used to be known as Bonnygate Church. The Scottish Episcopalian Church in St. Catherine Street, The Parish Church in the Kirkgate and St. John's in the Bonnygate remain the same.

Much has been done for the elderly in Cupar. The old Baptist building in the Provost Wynd has become the Age Concern Centre. Westport House at the Bonnygate end of North Union Street has now become a special living centre for the elderly. The residents have each their own flats but a caretaker with special qualifications is also in residence to look after the tenants. Westport House is council-controlled but a newly-opened independent residence for elderly citizens has been erected in the drive of what used to be Westfield House. This building also has a caretaker block. The well-equipped Adamson Hospital in the north of Cupar has now a fine health centre and geriatric wing. In the East Road a very modern home for the elderly was opened recently.

Regionalisation has created a great change in what used to be Fife's county town. At one time all roads led to Cupar but sadly it has now become a corridor town. At the moment its success seems to depend on tourism. Many attempts are being made to attract people to it at holiday times. Historically Cupar and the surrounding district offer much to the interested. It is a clean healthy little burgh, its buildings and lifestyle reflecting both the old and modern. There is a certain charm about its side streets and closes and the variety of building styles is an architectural interest.

In this ancient royal burgh there is something for everyone. Its many clubs cater for all age-groups. Young and old live amicably side by side as they have done throughout the centuries, taking the many changes through which the town has passed with courage and dauntless faith in the future.

1. An old picture of Cupar taken from the north of the town looking towards the south. The East Road is visible. Further round to the west is the Tontine Hotel and County Buildings. The tall spire is that of the fifteenth century tower of the Old Parish Church of Cupar. Just below it on elevated ground is Castlehill School or Madras Academy as it was known at the time of the picture.

2. This is a nineteenth century view of the East Road, Cupar, taken about the middle of the century. The houses on the right of the picture don't seem to have changed much over the years. To the extreme left is the jail, now the premises of Wm. Watt, seedsman. The old church spire is visible and further to the right is the cupola of Cupar Town Hall, the home of the Town Council. The Tontine Hotel and County Buildings are also visible. Opposite them is the Royal Hotel and further round to the right is Madras Academy.

3. The Neglected Children's Association, Cupar. This picture was taken by the Reverend Dr. Cochrane at the manse in the Millgate. The group is seated in the manse garden before breakfast. The members breakfasted monthly at each others' houses. The date of the picture is 1860. Sitting: Mr. J.M. Douglas, writer; Reverend Wm. Burnet, Boston Church; and Mr. Duncan, jeweller. Standing: Mr. Alex. Sharp, painter; Reverend Dr. Cochrane; Reverend Mr. Joseph, Baptist Church; Mr. Wm. Foote, draper; Mr. Simpson Philp, writer; Reverend John Rankine, Bonnygate (then Burnside) Church; and Mr. George Hogarth, banker.

4. Dr. Macdougall's English Class V in the Madras Academy, Cupar, in session 1877-78. Top row: John Prain (Cupar), John Beatson Bell (Belmore, Cupar), Henry McIntosh (Cupar), James Law (Kilmany) and Robert Hood (Cupar). Middle row: Archibald Maxwell (Balmalcolm, Kettle), David Brewster (Kilmany), William Walker (Kingask, Cupar), George L. Anderson (Ceres) and James Dryburgh (Kininmonth, Ceres) Front row: David Reid (Peasehills, Gauldry), Robert M. Adamson (Cupar), Robert Gordon Maxwell (Balmalcolm) and John Marshall (Cupar).

5. This is the old toll house on the Perth Road which was situated almost opposite the entrance to St. Mary's Road. The cottage is very old and is marked on Wood's map of 1820. Its date was probably late eighteenth century. It is an interesting cottage, so typical of its period. The dress of the two women is interesting also and so is the high pram. Unfortunately the cottage was demolished in the 1960's to make room for a school for specially handicapped children.

6. The 'Wet' Review of 1881. Cupar's representatives. Sitting: Messrs. Robert Aitchison, John Webster, Joseph Carscadden and William Aitchison. Standing: Walter Smith, Daniel McLeish, A. Allan, Robert Bett, Robert Dallas and George Howie.

7. Cupar Town Council in 1885. The photograph was taken by Mr. D. Gordon, photographer, Kirk Wynd, Cupar, in front of the Tontine Hotel, St. Catherine Street. In the centre front is Provost Hain, proprietor of the hotel. Some very important townspeople are in the photograph. The first gentleman in the front row, going left to right, is Mr. John Macqueen, afterwards Provost, proprietor of the Royal Hotel. Beside him is Mr. Thomas Malcolm Gray, Barony, afterwards Dean of Guild and Honorary Sheriff. Seated to the left of Provost Hain is Bailie Honeyman, Craigmore. On the other side of him is Bailie Rutherford, proprietor of Waterloo Tavern, afterwards Provost. On the extreme left of Provost Hain is Mr. W. Duncan, jeweller, St. Catherine Street (before Mr. T.L. Brown). The gentleman with the beard, fourth from the left in the back row is Mr. George Robertson, jeweller, Bonnygate, county inspector of weights and measures. Sixth from the left in the back row is Mr. John Innes, founder of the Cupar firm of printers and publishers. Eighth from the left of the back row is Mr. Thomas Davidson, burgh procurator-fiscal, and beside him his elder son, Mr. R.J. Davidson, then a town councillor. The kilted figure in the back row is Walter Paul, town officer.

8. Cupar Bakers, 1887, on parade in Cupar during the town's celebrations for Queen Victoria's Silver Jubilee.

Crossgate, Cupar

9. A picture of the Crossgate, Cupar, in the 1890's. Coming down towards the turning into South Bridge at the Station Hotel is the town's horse-drawn cab with its liveried driver. This form of local transport began on 22nd May 1866. The cab and cabbie were a familiar sight well into the first quarter of the twentieth century. There must still be many townspeople who saw it as it waited for passengers going or coming by train, at Cupar Station.

CROSSGATE, CUPAR

10. This is the Station Hotel Corner in the 1890's. Formerly the hotel was called the Bluebell Inn. The Crossgate was cobbled as were all the main streets in the town. Looking across the street from the Station Hotel the entrance to the Short Lane can be seen at the right hand side of which is the Waterloo Tavern. Looking up the Crossgate can be seen the spire of the Duncan Institute on the left hand side. Further north can be seen the cupola of the Town Hall and towering behind is the spire of the Corn Exchange.

11. This is a view of the Bonnygate, looking west in the 1890's. The transport is horse-drawn. On the right can be seen the milk cart going its rounds. There is quite a variety of colour in the stonework of the houses on the right. Just before St. John's Church is the tall building with darkish pink-coloured stone. This used to be the residence in early days of Doctor Charles Grace, son-in-law of the reverend Dr. Campbell of the Old Parish Church. Marathon House can be seen just beyond St. John's, the residence of Dr. MacDonald. The spire in the far distance is that of St. Michael's Church, towering above Mrs. Kellie's shop at Westport.

BONNYGATE CUPAR

12. This is the narrow neck of the Bonnygate in the 1890's. The boy with the bicycle and his friend are standing at the entrance to Balmerino Place which in days long past was the winter residence of Lord Balmerino. On the left hand side of the street is the striking building belonging to Mr. Campbell, the fishmonger (now the business of Mr. Montador). The stonework is of a rich red colour and the tower with the flagstaff makes it one of the most impressive buildings in the town. Further west, on the right side, is the spire of Bonnygate Church and away in the distance is the spire of St. Michael's Church.

13. This picture is taken in the Bonnygate. The church is the Bonnygate Church and the premises beside it belong to Mr. Edmund, the baker. Mr. and Mrs. Edmund are standing at the door of the shop and two young employees are standing at the entrance to the bakehouse. This shop was later demolished to make an entrance to Bonnygate Manse which was erected behind the church.

This is St. John's Church in the Bonnygate, erected in 1878. It took the place of the first 'Free Presbyterian Church' in Union Street (Mews Wynd), the congregation of which came together after the Disruption of 1843. St. John's was made possible by money given for the purpose by Sir David Baxter of Kilmaron Castle. Behind the church on the left hand side can be seen the manse of Bonnygate Church.

14. This scene is taken at the top of Wemysshall Hill. The first half of the picture shows the column of Cupar's Old Mercat Cross with the unicorn on top which has lost its horn. The Cross had been removed from its central position in the town in 1812 and five years later, in 1817, the laird of Wemysshall had it sunk into a cairn of stones on an elevated site on his estate. In 1897 he gave permission to Provost McQueen to have it brought back to the town and erected at the top of the Crossgate in honour of Queen Victoria's Diamond Jubilee. The second half of the picture shows the column and unicorn safely removed and lying in the straw-strewn lorry at Wemysshall Hill. The work was done by the late Mr. Houston of Hillside Foundry and he can be seen standing on the lorry.

The Barracks, Cupar.

15. During the years between Provost Ferguson's demolition of the old Tolbooth in Cupar in 1813 and the election of the Fife Prison Board, the prison in Cupar was the building which eventually became the business premises of Messrs. Watt, seedsman. This prison, however, was never satisfactory and it was decided to find a new site for a jail of about two to six acres, about one and a half miles from the Court Room at Cupar. The site decided upon was in the north-east of the Braehead district. The foundation stone was laid on 27th September 1842 and the building was finished in 1843. It continued as a jail until 1888 when it became a military barracks. During the Second World War it was used as a prison again by the Polish Forces stationed in Cupar area. The walls are very strong and it is their structural strength that has made demolition almost impossible and so the building has survived. It was from this building that the Scanlan brothers were taken to the Fluthers to be hanged for murder on 5th July 1852, the last public hanging to take place in the town.

16. This photograph shows the rejoicing in Cupar on the relief of Mafeking 1900. Some of the figures can be recognised. The constable with his back to us is Ex-Sergeant Coventry, later a bailie in Auchtermuchty. Beside him is Sergeant Martin whose 'silent tread' made not a few boys take 'leg bail' thirty years ago. Mr Lewis Graham in cricket flannels is standing beside Mr. Brown Murray, one of the sons of a former minister of Dairsie. Mr. Graham was a well-loved schoolmaster in the town who set many a Castlehill lad on the right road to learning.

17. This is South Bridge in 1900. In the foreground to the left is the Station Hotel, once the Bluebell Inn. The station lies ahead. The first attempt at constructing a railway in Fife was made in 1841 when the Edinburgh and Northern Railway Company was formed. In 1847 a line from Burntisland to Cupar was completed and a year later a line from Cupar to Newport was opened. A railway bridge for the town was achieved for Cupar through the energies of Mr. Makgill Crichton whose statue can be seen near the top of the bridge.

BELL-BAXTER SCHOOL AND WESTPORT, CUPAR

18. Bell Baxter School and Westport, Cupar. This is a picture of Bell Baxter School as it used to be until 1932 when an extension was added. It was erected in 1870 by money gifted by Lady Baxter of Kilmaron Castle. It was originally called the Baxter Institution for Young Ladies. The school was successfully conducted by a series of headmistresses, the last of whom was Miss Peacock. She had the coveted privilege of being granted the County Hall for her annual concert and exhibition. When she had to vacate the Baxter Institution in 1889, she moved to Weston House opposite, the cobbled entrance to which is seen in the picture. The 'Bell' part of Bell Baxter was added in 1890, the result of the endowment of Dr. Andrew Bell of St. Andrews and Madras, India, where his educational system was so renowned that it was adopted in this country. Further east, adjacent to the school, is St. Michael's Church, erected in 1837 to accommodate the over-spill at the Old Parish Church in the Kirkgate. The house beyond the church with the whitish walls was the home of the Duffus family which gave Cupar its beautiful park and sports facilities.

PARISH CHURCH AND KIRKGATE, CUPAR, FIFE

19. This is a picture of the Parish Church and Kirkgate looking from the west. The entrance to the left in the foreground leads to South Union Street (Mews Wynd). The entrance to the right of the picture leads into Lovers' Lane. The little shop at the corner of Lovers' Lane was a delight to all five to seven year olds attending Kirkgate School in Lovers' Lane who had a penny to spend. The Kirkgate at the time of the picture was cobbled and it had a peacefulness which modern times have quite taken away from it. The church tower is the oldest building in the town, its date being 1415. The church of St. Christopher to which it belongs was rather thoughtlessly demolished to make way for the present 1785 building. When it was built, the tower was square at the top, but one of the ministers of the old church, the Reverend Will Scott, had the additional spire erected at his own expense during his ministry in the seventeenth century.

20. This is the Fife Herald and Journal shop at 8 Bonnygate which was the property bought by Robert Tullis when he came to Cupar in 1800. Tullis had trained as a printer, bookbinder and bookseller and it was at 8 Bonnygate that he set up a shop in the front and a printing press behind. He himself lived in the flat above. He earned a high reputation for his publishing work and in 1822 founded the first Fife County newspaper, the 'Fife Herald', the first number of which was published on 14th March 1822, printed on hand-made paper from his mill at Auchmuty.

Tannery & North Burnside, Cupar, Fife.

21. The Tannery and North Burnside, Cupar about 1900. The Tannery was one of Cupar's oldest businesses. The first owner was Mr. Honeyman, a brother of Mr. John Honeyman of the South Bridge Linen Works. Mr. Honeyman's successor was the firm of Messrs. James Carmichael & Sons Ltd. Dundee which took over about the beginning of the present century. For two or three decades it was a most successful business but about the middle of the century motorisation on farms saw a decrease in the demand for harness leather and it was with great reluctance that the Tannery closed down in May, 1951. In the distance can be seen the Gasworks which supplied gas to the town for the first time on 3rd January, 1831. The streets of Cupar were first lighted by gas on 2nd February, 1831.

22. Westfield House is one of the most attractive houses in Cupar and it has an historical significance for it was once a girls' day and board-ing school run by Miss Henrietta Keddie and her sister, daughters of a well-known lawyer in Cupar, in the first decades of the nineteenth century. The sisters opened their school first in what is known as the Chancellor's House in the Crossgate about 1858 but in the 1860s they moved to Westfield House, the front of which is seen in the photograph. The main entrance to it was in the west of the Bonnygate almost opposite Hill Street. There was a lodge, and a drive led up to the house. Miss Henrietta Keddie who became a writer of no little repute with a large number of novels to her credit, was in charge of the establishment which she describes in her book 'Three Generations'. The front of the house faced the south and a wooden door led on to Westfield Road. The lodge was demolished after the Second World War and its site and the drive taken over as a garage and lock-ups. Recently the ground has become the site of an independent housing scheme for the elderly. The house is still inhabited and the school bell is in the ownership of the last proprietor.

THE CROSS AND ST. CATHERINE STREET, CUPAR

23. This is a picture of the Mercat Cross and St. Catherine Street, Cupar, taken about 1900. Notice the cobbled streets. The Mercat Cross is back in all its glory. It is surrounded by four gas lamps. There is also a drinking fountain and two convenient steps for reaching it. To the right of the Mercat Cross, above Galloway's Hat and Cap Warehouse, are the windows of the Town Hall, the meeting place of the Town Council. The flat above accommodates Town Council staff. To the left of the Cross can be seen the entrance to the hill on which stands Castlehill School and beyond are bank buildings, the Episcopalian Chapel, St. James' and the Royal Hotel. On the other side of the street are the County Buildings. St. Catherine Street, so called because of the monastery that was there in mediaeval times, stretches down to the Haugh. There was no War Memorial until 1922.

CUPAR FROM EDEN

24. This is a view of Cupar from the Eden. On the right hand side is the Haugh. The spire straight in front is that of the Parish Church. To the right are the spires of the Corn Exchange and St. John's Church.

25. The old industry of pipe-clay making was established in Cupar about the middle of the 19th century by the grandfather of Mr. James Burton. He was the only clay-pipe maker north of the Forth. The industry started in the Hedging Close in Cupar about 1835 but moved to Back Lebanon in 1849. The clay for the pipes was imported from Devonshire. The picture shows Mr. Mitchell at work in the premises at Back Lebanon. The average output of a clay-pipe worker was eighteen dozen pipes an hour and about twelve gross per day. At one time the industry turned out 150 gross per week.

26. The home hole at Cupar Golf Course taken about 1900.
The Greenkeeper at Hilltarvit Golf Course. The picture was taken
in 1906.

27. This is a picture of the premises of the Danish Produce Company at 35 Bonnygate about 1900. Today the same premises house the business of Messrs. Hood and Walker.

28. This is a photograph of Castlehill School Staff taken in 1901. Back row: Sergeant Stott, Mr. W.S. Davidson, Mrs. Buchanan (Miss Wann), Mr. Nairn, Mrs. Ritchie (Miss Bella Wood) and John A.D. Ross. Middle row: Mr. D. Duke, Miss Beveridge, Mr. Thom, headmaster; Mrs. Stanford (Miss Walker) and Mr. W.H. Simpson, art master. Front row: Miss Beatrice Stowell, Miss James and Miss Eva Jeffrey.

29. In 1900 Cupar footballers won the Davidson Cup. Here is the team in 1902; the names are: back: R. Dick, A. Mitchell, Duncan McAndrew and T.S. Porter. Middle: A. Watson, George Fettes, George Stewart, R. Campbell and William Douglas. Front: Alex. Young, Robert Robertson and Leonard Wallace.

A Cupar Rink of Curlers at Tailabout, 1902. Left to right: J. Young, J. Mitchell Ramsay, A.F. Finch, R. Dott Thomson, J. Mackie, T. Wilkie, George Harris and Bailie Brown.

30. The proclamation of the succession to the throne of King George V took place at the Mercat Cross, Cupar, on 10th May 1910. This was just the second occasion on which a succeeding monarch had been proclaimed at the Mercat Cross since its return in 1897 from Wemysshall Hill. The first was that of Edward VII in 1901.

31. Here are 'General' Gordon and Jimmie Dickie, harmless Cupar worthies of the 1890's. They were the successors of 'Coorse' Ritchie, Jock Bowse and Tiger Suttie of still older times. There are no such characters in the town today. There are no horses' heads to hold on a Tuesday as of old, and the harmless class who provided a butt for many a wag is now no more.

32. This is the late Provost MacQueen, Cupar, as he appeared at Queen Victoria's Diamond Jubilee in London in 1897. It was Provost MacQueen who had the old Mercat Cross returned to the centre of the royal burgh after an absence of eighty-five years, in honour of the Queen's long reign of sixty years.

33. Ambulance Class, 'K' Coy., 6th Volunteer Battalion, Royal Highlanders, Cupar, 1902. Back row: Privates W.O. Nicoll, C.C. Edmond, A. Porter, W. Howie (Bugler), J. Taylor, G. Whillans, J. Mitchell, A. Wood, H.T. Reidie, W. Oxlade and D.G. Mackie. Front row: Sergeant T. Batchelor, Colour-Sergeant Instructor W. Ross, R.M.L.I., Lieutenant T.J. Robertson, Surgeon-Major C.E. Douglas, Colour-Sergeant R. Bett, Sergeant W. Peggie and Private T. Crombie.

34. Cupar Town Band, 1902. Back row: J. Cunningham, Ex-Councillor T. Menzies, D. Keiller, E. Fraser, R. Brown, J. White, D. Stuart, W. Scott, G. Jamieson and Bailie Arnot. Front row: James Mitchell, A. Dowie, A. Todd, A. McBayne (Bandmaster), John Mitchell, A. Allison and F. Soutar.

35. This is Mr. James Duffus, elder son of Mr. James Duffus, Westport House, Cupar, who died suddenly on 1st May 1904, at the age of 54. Educated at the old Madras Academy, he got his early training under Messrs. Grummond, jute manufacturer, Dundee, after which he was sent as representative to Calcutta. After a prosperous career, he joined with his younger brother John and between them they set up a fine business which had, eventually, the largest turn-over in the jute trade in Britain. They never forgot their home town and it was Mr. John Duffus who donated so much money towards the Duffus Park and its recreational facilities.

36. The Adamson Cottage Hospital, Cupar, 1904, was made possible by money left by Mr. Alexander Adamson for a small hospital in Ceres. Owing to the inaccessibility of Ceres the trustees decided to combine with various benevolent societies in Cupar and the hospital in the north of the royal burgh was the result. Owing to the generosity of Mr. & Mrs. Crichton of Luthriebank who gifted over £5,000 for extensions and furnishings as well as a bond of annuity for seven years of £1,500, the hospital became one of the finest Cottage Hospitals in Scotland. New wings were added. X-Ray apparatus was made possible by a gift from Mrs. Ferric of Parbroath and a further gift from Lord and Lady Cochrane of Cults secured diathermy and violet ray apparatus. This photograph of the Hospital was taken in January 1929 after it was re-opened with the extensions.

37. Cupar Cattle Show, 18th June 1904. The picture shows the officials at the Grand Stand. Front row, left to right: W. Guild, Lindores; A. Buttercase, Uthrogle; Captain Gilmour, Woodburne; G. Russell, Hatton; R.G. Fortune, Rosebank and J. Borrowman, veterinary surgeon, Cupar. Second row: D. Ferguson, Foxton, the late Colonel Anstruther-Thomson; Sir John Gilmour, Major W. Anstruther-Gray (President) and Sir Ralph Anstruther. Third row: George Innes (Fife Herald and Journal); G. Gilroy, Rankeilour; J. Miller, Nydie Mains; A. Orchison, Torr o' Moonzie; Mr. Taylor, Mullingar, Ireland; A. Lawson, Annfield; D. Ferrie, Parbroath; W. Marshall, Lochmalony; Andrew Smith, Waltonhill; J.L. Brown, Cupar; Major Scott-Davidson, Cairnie; F.W. Christie, Dairsie Mains (Secretary); and Mr. Roger, Balgove. In Grand Stand behind centre of third row is Mr. Bell, Todhall.

38. Cupar Rugby Club, 1905-1906. Back row: A.H. Symon, D.H. Shaw, C. Drysdale, J. Crawford, T. Critchley, T. Hutchison, James Stewart, S. Millie, G.S. Fairweather, J. Myles, E. Walton and A.C. Clapperton. In front: J. Clark, J.W. Ritch, C.W. Russell, R. Robertson and J. Hill.

39. Sir Thomas Barclay, LL.B., Ph.D. was the eldest son of Mr. George Barclay, laird of Bonvil, Cupar. Educated at Madras Academy, Cupar, in France, and at the University of Jena he became a barrister in 1881. In 1899 he became President of the British Chamber in Paris. He strove to improve relations between France and Great Britain and was awarded a knighthood in 1914 and later an officership of the Legion of Honour. At the death of his father at Bonvil, Mr. John Duffus bought the mansion and grounds and gifted them to Cupar Town Council.

40. This picture is of the Bonnygate, looking down towards the narrow neck of the street. Marathon House, the residence of Dr. MacDonald, has a prominent place in the view. Beside it stands Bonnygate Church, now the Baptist Church, and further on at the left hand side can be seen the railings of St. John's Church. The interesting feature of this picture is the weeding of the cobbled street which is being done by three women who are down on their knees, pulling out the unsightly weeds. This was a common sight last century and during the early years of the present century. Women were paid for doing this work. The date of this picture is 1906.

Cupar. Old Tower and Church

ARTYR'S MONUMENT, OLD CHURCHYARD, CUPAR.

41. This is the old tower and Parish Church in Cupar. The tower dates from 1415 and was part of the first church in the Kirkgate dedicated to St. Christopher. It was a large building which was said to have been as big as Glasgow Cathedral. The roof had been greatly neglected and instead of trying to repair the damage, those responsible pulled down the building and built a new church which was opened for worship in 1785. The only parts of the original building are the tower and part of the session house which are visible in the picture.

This is the Martyr's Monument in the old churchyard behind the Parish Church in the Kirkgate. There is writing on both sides of the tombstone which are shown on the postcard. Cupar has a special interest in David Hackston whose estate just lay a few miles to the north of Cupar at Rathillet. The seventeenth century building which was his home is part of the steading at Rathillet farm now. Hackston was most cruelly murdered for his part in the Covenanting Movement in Scotland in the seventeenth century. Parts of his dismembered body were sent all over the country to act as a deterrent to others who followed his example. It was one of his hands that was interred in the tomb in the churchyard in the Kirkgate. At one time the Parish minister held an annual service at the tomb on the Sunday in July nearest the date of Hackston's death. On that day special flowers brought from Rathillet were laid at the foot of the tombstone.

42. Cupar Ornithological Society's Office-bearers and Members of Committee for 1906. Back row, left to right: James Speed, John Goodfellow, P. Ruddiman, A. Allan, T. Speed, D. Smith, D.J. Bruce, Andrew Brass and J. MacPherson. Centre row: D. Donaldson, senior: D. Edmund, W. Ruddiman (Secretary and Treasurer), T. Gibson (Vice-President), Bailie Simpson (Honorary Vice-President), G. White, (President), D. Robertson, C.C. Edmund, senior (Vice-President) and C. Welch. Front row: C.C. Edmund, junior; D. Donaldson, junior; W. McIntosh, R. Drysdale, R. Houston, J. Dick, J. Low, J. Drysdale and T. Simpson, junior.

43. Suffragettes in Cupar. This picture was taken during the suffragettes campaign in the East Fife constituency in September 1906. The picture shows Miss Teresa Billington addressing a meeting at the Cross, Cupar, and occupying the lorry behind are Miss Christabel Pankhurst and Miss Annie Kenny.

East Bridge and Carthaugh, Cupar

44. East Bridge and Cartaugh, Cupar. This picture is dated 1907. On the right hand side is the Fluthers and the opening leads up to Castlefield and the Old Jail. Straight ahead can be seen the road leading into the Burnside and further on can be seen the lane that leads up to Castlehill. The cupola and spire of the Town Hall stand out and on the extreme right is the spire of the Corn Exchange. In between the two spires is Castlehill School, somewhat obscured by trees.

SIMPSON BRIDGE, CUPAR.

45. The Simpson Bridge stands south of Cupar Muir. There has been a bridge there since the eighteenth century and for thirty years previous to 1902 the Walker Bridge stood there. The Walker Bridge had previously spanned the Eden opposite South Bridge Works, but Mr. James Walker, writer, collected subscriptions to have it re-erected near Tarvit Mill. The winter floods of 1902 carried the wooden erection away and for months those who had made frequent use of the bridge bemoaned its absence. Ex-Bailie Simpson was then a Town Councillor and a man of great energy. He set about collecting money to replace the bridge. The old Guildry Fund supplied a nucleus of £50 and the Bailie soon got promises of another £50 from Cupar people at home and abroad. The late Mr. Thomas Aitken, road surveyor, designed and supervised the erection of the present structure, and on 10th October 1903, the late Honorary Sheriff Honeyman cut the ribbon and declared the bridge open. In recognition of his valuable services the bridge was named after Ex-Bailie Simpson.

46. This is St. Catherine Street, Cupar, looking east, as it was in 1909. On the right hand side is the Royal Hotel and next to it is the Episcopal Church. Adjoining the church are the Clydesdale and British Linen Banks. The entrance to Castlehill School is visible and towering above is the spire of the Corn Exchange. Away beyond in the Bonnygate is the spire of Bonnygate Church, now the Baptist Church. The old Mercat Cross is not very clear on the card. On the left hand side of the picture opposite the Royal Hotel, are the County Buildings.

South Road, Cupar.

47. South Road, Cupar, about 1910.

48. This is a group of Girl Guides at Cupar, about 1910, when the first Company was formed.

49. A group of senior pupils taken outside the headmaster's room or board room at Castlehill School in 1915. The headmaster, standing to the right of the pupils, is Mr. David Struth, B.A., who was to become one of Cupar's provosts in later years.

Castlehill School as it looked in the 1890's. The old Burgh School of 1727 is exactly opposite the entrance gate. The right hand side of the building is quite different from what it is today. The large building on the right is a nineteenth century extension. The two cottages had nothing to do with the school. A roadway ran down between them and the 1727 building called 'The Wynd'. Later, after the 1908 Education Act, the cottages were removed and the ground was used as a further extension for the school.

FLOOD. BURNSIDE CUPAR. .8.7.16

50. The Burnside in flood, 8th July 1916. During the time of the rain storm, boats were used to ferry grown ups and school children from one side of the Burnside to the other. The steep rise of the Newtown is seen between Mr. Aitcan's bread shop and the houses on the other side.

HAUGH FROZEN OVER 1916

51. On the ice at Cupar. This picture is taken of the Haugh in the winter of 1916. Soldiers can be seen mingling with the townsfolk. Cupar was always well-known for its skaters. The flooded Haugh was an ideal place for those inclined to this form of sport. On such occasions Bell Baxter pupils were allowed to indulge this inclination when severe frosty weather conditions debarred them from the usual winter school sports of hockey and rugby.

52. Tea-tent workers at Sports held in aid of Soldiers' Comforts at Kinloss, on 12th August 1916.

53. Flax pickers at Pitscottie, 1916. During the First World War farmers in Cupar District grew a large acreage of flax for the manufacture of linen cloth. The bright blue flowers of the flax fields made a pretty sight in the summer time. It was harvested in the autumn and the work was done to a great extent by volunteer workers, quite a number of these being women as most men were servicing in the Forces.

CIVIC GUARD IN TRAINING.

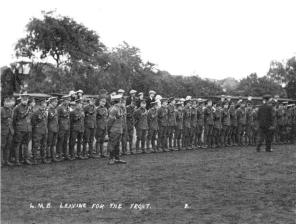

L.M.B. LEAVING FOR THE FRONT.

L.M.B. LEAVING FOR THE FRONT.

54. Although it says 'Cupar Civic Guard in training' on the post-card, the term 'Local Defence Volunteers' seems to have been the better known to describe townsmen who for various reasons were not accepted for the Forces. These volunteers, however, did valuable work and were trained for special constable duties during the First World War. Here the Cupar Volunteers are training in the Carthaugh. They did not have a special uniform but they wore arm bands with the letters C.G. on them.

Troops of the Lowland Mounted Brigade lined up in the Carthaugh, about to leave for the Front during the First World War.

The Lowland Mounted Brigade, 1914, on the station platform at Cupar, ready to board the train. Friends and relatives are gathered to see them off.

Railway Station, Cupar

55. The railway station, Cupar. The date of the picture is 1918.

56. On 10th May 1919, Earl Haig was made a Freeman of the burgh. The ceremony took place in St. John's Church. In this picture taken at the church door, Earl Haig can be seen standing beside Provost Stark. Others in the group are Sir William Robertson, Lord Lieutenant of Fife, Sheriff Principal Fleming, Sir Ralph Anstruther, Bart., and Colonel Alexander Sprot, M.P.

This was the arch at the Station Hotel corner, erected as a welcome to Earl Haig as he walked at the head of the procession which made its way into the Crossgate and the Bonnygate to St. John's Church where the Freedom Ceremony took place.

THE BONNYGATE, CUPAR.

57. The Bonnygate, Cupar, 1920. The age of the car has made its appearanc

58. Cupar Golf Club, 1920. Members are gathered together outside the clubhouse at Hilltarvit.

59. Cupar Football Team, 1920. Back row, left to right: Moyes, J. Georgeson, Martin, H. Crawford, McPherson, J. Brown and Haxton. Second row: D. Rodger, J. Donaldson, G. Philip, T. Doig and A. Donaldson. In front: B. Donaldson.

Crossgate, Cupar.

M. 357.

60. The Crossgate, Cupar, 1920.

61. Tarvit House, Cupar, 1920. The last laird of this lovely mansion was Major Lumsden. After the Second World War it was demolished to make room for the new housing estates that have been erected in that area. The estate was formerly called Nether Tarvit to distinguish it from the estate of Upper Tarvit (later Wemysshall). Early in the 17th century it belonged to the Sibbalds of Gibliston. In 1720 it was acquired by James Rigg of Downfield who was descended from the old Fifeshire family of Rigg of Aithernie.

62. War Memorial, Cupar, 1922. This impressive memorial was unveiled on 29th April 1922 by Earl Haig. The designer of the angel was Mr. H.S. Garnley, R.S.A., an Edinburgh designer of some repute. The pedestal on which the statue stood was the work of Mr. John Kinross, R.S.A., also of Edinburgh. He was also responsible for the bronze panels with the engraven names and he also designed the iron railing which was moulded by Messrs. Smith and Wellstood, Edinburgh and London. The railing was given special applications of paint by Mr. Chalmers, the new painter in the Burnside. The mason work for the Memorial was carried out by Mr. R.G. Finlay, builder, Cupar. The granolithic stairs were made by Messrs. Stewart & Company, Edinburgh.

The Guard of Honour at the unveiling of the War Memorial. Left to right: J.O. Ramsay, A. Gordon, J. Bett, T. Lumsden and D. Anderson.

63. Cupar Rugby Club, season 1928-29. Standing, left to right: E.J. French, D. Weir, P.C. Jack, W. Geddes, D. Traill, J.L. Smart, H.L. Stewart, A.C.F. Ness, G. Wilson and H.G. Birrell. Sitting: W. Edie, M. McKenzie, T. McKinlay, A. Todd and G. White.

64. Cupar Cubs with Cub Mistress Lumsden, 8th June 1919. This picture was taken at a splendid rally of Boy Scouts in Cupar at which these youngsters entered enthusiastically into the afternoon's work.

65. Cupar Bowling Green was in excellent condition in 1928 when many games were played. The picture shows some of the 'big men' of the Club. Left to right: T. Durie, M. Gorrie, R.G. Finlay, J. Dickie, W. Boyd and W. Williamson.

Kilmaron Castle, Cupar

66. Kilmaron Castle, although only of nineteenth century vintage, was, until its demolition in the summer of 1983, one of the most elegant and pleasant mansions in the neighbourhood of Cupar. It was built from design by Gillespie Graham, the famous architect, for Admiral Maitland, a renowned naval officer, a son of Over Rankeilour. It had a commanding site in the area and was visible from a great distance. The castle's next owner was Mr. James Cheyne who lived in it until 1856 when it was purchased by Sir David Baxter, Bart., of Dundee. At Sir David's death in 1872 the castle passed to a nephew who never stayed in it. For a time it was rented to tenants by the Baxter family. Eventually it passed into the ownership of Sir James Low whose family lived in it until 1983. It was at that date the residence of a grandson of Sir James Low who sadly had to demolish the building for safety reasons. Sir James Morrison-Low, however, still resides near the site of the castle in a fine modern, commodious bungalow where he upholds the traditions of his family.

67. Mr. James Bonnar was the son of Dr. George Lindsay Bonnar, a medical practitioner in Cupar in the late 1880's. After training in the flax industry he went to South Africa to join his father there. He took up farming with his brother in Natal and later served in the Boer War. Returning to Cupar in 1907, he purchased Glendura, at 112 Bonnygate, formerly occupied by his aunt, Miss Margaret Walker. Taking a great interest in the town's activities, he became interested in collecting articles connected with Cupar in olden days. He established the museum at Castlehill School which was later transferred to the Duncan Institute. Mr. Bonnar died at Glendura on 15th August 1930, aged 81.

68. The House Party at Crawford Priory at the Celebration of the golden wedding of Lord and Lady Cochrane, on 2nd December 1930. Seated: Major the Hon. T.G.F. Cochrane, D.S.O. (eldest son), Lady Cochrane of Cults, Lord Cochrane of Cults (with Cairn Terrier), Countess of Elgin (daughter). Standing: Sir Thomas Fowell Buxton (son-in-law), Lady Newton, Earl of Dundonald (brother of Lord Cochrane), the Hon. Mrs. Leith-Hay, Earl of Elgin and Kincardine, C.M.G. (son-in-law), Commander the Hon. A.D. Cochrane, D.S.O. (son), Hon. Mrs. A.D. Cochrane.

69. Cupar and District Pipe Band in the mid-1920's. The band was formed in 1920 and very soon became a recognised institution in the district. The founder was Mr. L. McLaren who is seen sitting with the drum in front of him.

70. Cupar Brownie Pack, 1930. Back row, left to right: Pack Leader K. Fairbairn, Tawny Owl D. Robertson, Brown Owl A. Hogg and Pack Leader H.J. Heron. Second row: N. Simpson, A. Mudie, J. Ramsay, N. Wrather, M. Johnston, A. Donaldson, M. Low and B. Low. Third row: S. White, B. Chalmers, I. Johnston, S. Davidson, J. Ironside and J. Grant. Front row: R. Noble, B. Alexander, B. Johnston and N. Wrather.

71. The children of St. John's Church Junior Choir, Cupar, who performed the Japanese operetta, 'Princess Chrysanthemum' in 1930. Miss G.M. Gorrie L.R.A.M. the conductor, is seen on the extreme left. Back row: N. Forrest, J. Denholm, I. Halcro, N. Reid and I. Peebles. Second row: G. Douglas, N. Little, B. Hutton, C. Kinnear and I. Fisher. Third row: E. Pearson, M. Houston, M. Douglas, H. Kerr (Princess Chrysanthemum), J. Reid (Emperor What-for-whi), I. Burnett, I. Brown, D. Reid and M. Little. Front row: I. Carver, A. Peebles, S. Kinnear, D. White, J. Browning (Saucer Eyes), J. Donaldson, P. White, I. Kane, M. Fisher and P. Denholm.

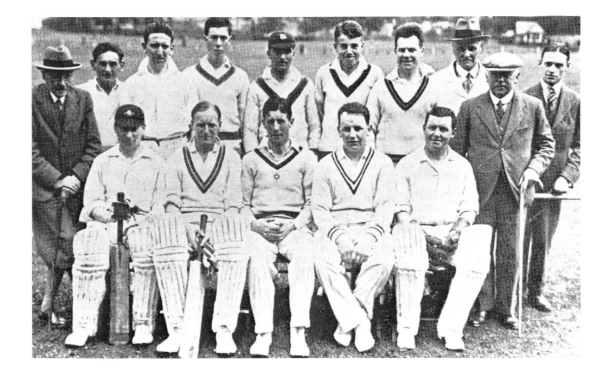

72. Cupar Cricket Club, season 1931. Standing: Dr. C.E. Douglas (Vice-President), T.A. Barclay, F. Campbell, D. Bell, Clowes (prof.), W.R. Heggie, A.A. Lumsden, P. Hutton (Umpire), Mr. Charles Cairns (Vice-President) and C.D. Pagan (Hon. Joint Secretary). Seated: D. White, H.L. Stewart (Vice-Captain), J.D. Graeme Reid (Captain), D. Craig and C.C. Edmond.

73. First Cupar Company of the Boys'.Brigade photographed afer the dedication service in Bonnygate Church, on 8th November 1931. The Chaplain, the Reverend R.D.M. Johnston, is seen in the centre. On his right are Captain J.B. Russell and Staff Sergeant S. Bell, and on his left are Lieutenant J.O. Paul and Sergeant D. Brown.

74. Cupar Scouts in the 1930's. Front row: W. Maxwell, E. McColm, W. Jordan, T.L.G. Green, R.L.J.M. Lindsay, S.M.D. Fleming, A.S.M.J. Brownlie, A. Duncan, R. Halliday and A. Yates. Second row: Sec. J. Halliday, J. Bain, R. Wallace, G. Simpson, I. Davidson, W. Wilson, M. Small, Sec. J. Duncan and Sec. T. Henderson. Third row: A. Boyd, M. Magee, Sec. R. Fleming and P.L.H. Anderson. Fourth row: P.L.I. Burnett, W. Boyd and J. Brook. Flag bearers: P.L.W. Green and P.L.J. Michie. The flags were presented by Mr. J. Brown, Millbank, Cupar.

75. Cupar lady tennis players in the 1930's. Members of the Cupar Duffus Tennis Club's Ladies' Team who played in the Second Division of the Midland League last season. In front: Miss E. Davidson, Mrs. H.J. French and Miss Mary Stewart. At back: Miss May Carver, Miss E.B. Stewart and Miss Nora French.

76. Kinnear House Kindergarten in the 1930's. Miss S. Robertson (mistress), Allan Simpson, Neil Innes, Kirsty Macdonald, Kathleen Bonar, Patricia Watt, Patrick Hendry, Ian McMurray, Ismay Kerr, Billy Boyd and Ronald McMurray.

77. In January 1929, the Adamson Cottage Hospital was re-opened with the extensions made possible by the generosity of Mr. and Mrs. Crichton of Luthriebank. Lord Cochrane of Cults performed the opening ceremony before a large and representative gathering. Left to right: Dr. Robertson, Dr. MacDonald, Dr. McLeish, Miss Stark (matron), Provost Smith, Mr. J.B. Crichton, Lord Cochrane, Dr. Douglas, Lady Cochrane and Mr. T.W. Davidson.

78. Fife Beekeepers in the early 1930's. Standing, left to right: The Reverend R. Alexander, Cupar (President), Mr. D.M. Rollo, Cupar (Honorary Secretary and Treasurer), Mrs. Robertson, Edinburgh and Mr. W. Reid (Ex-President), holding a cup he presented to the Association for annual competition

79. Cupar Fire Brigade (1930's) with their up-to-date engine have proved their worth on several occasions at fires in the district. They can always be relied upon for a speedy 'turn-out', and, given a plentiful water supply, they can quickly subdue the flames. Back row: G.O.H. Grant (driver), D. McIntosh, W. Roḑger and W. Smith, junior. Standing: Councillor J. Taylor (convener), R. Bett, T. Smith, D. Macdonald (firemaster), G. Smith and L. Wilson. In front: D. Reid and H. Yule.